Dedicated to a great Pink Floyd fan, Pino Imparato, passed away too early.

Collecting Japan Editions

The nicest Pink Floyd's editions are surely the Japanese ones, because of the presence of the ideograms and of the OBI on them.

What is an OBI ?

In the beginning, an OBI was a paper strip of about 2" wrapped around the LP covers, with the name of the artist, record and song's title, price in Yen and other information written on it in Japanese.

On CDs the OBI is a piece of paper that wraps the jewel case from left to back for about 1" each side, still with the same information provided for an LP.

A Japanese edition is considered incomplete without the OBI, and its value decreases.

The Issues

In Japan, Pink Floyd's Vinyl editions did go through 3 big phases: Odeon, EMI, and Sony. Let's analyze each one of them separately.

Odeon

Those are the very first issues, between '67 and '73, from "The piper at the gates of dawn" to "The dark side of the moon" included, plus "The Madcap Laughs" and "Barrett" by Syd Barrett and "Music from the Body" by Roger Waters.

The catalogue numbers looks like OP-xxxx for the very first prints and OP-yyyyy for the other ones. Lately was added an "E" in front during transition from Odeon to EMI (for EP, they use OR as prefix).

For the OP-xxxxx series, 2 different editions exist, the original and the reprint, which differ for the price on obi (2000 vs. 2200 Yen) and the presence of * or ** on the label. Also, up to '71 some copies was print in Rubin red transparent color, not intentionally to be a colored issue, but because the use of a special vinyl with anti-static properties, that bring that color.

Stock copies had black labels, sample copies had white label.

EMI

Between '74 and '78 the same titles as Odeon was reprint under EMI with red/tan label color, sample was black/white. In 1988 was also printed a HiFi version of "The dark side of the moon" (ProUse) and a club edition with totally different cover, with a photo taken from live performance, soon retired and became one of the rare pieces to collect.

Sony

Sony took over EMI from '75 to '87, from "Wish you were here" to "a Momentary Lapse of reason" and solos records for same period.

Conclusion
Collecting Japanese Pink Floyd editions is expensive but rewarding. I hope to contribute the knowledge of people who want to share same interest.

Credits
The photos in this book are 99% from my private collection, with a small percentage taken from Internet and some friends (Adriano Rizzi, Alberto Santoro).
A special thanks to Alessandro Mario Montoli for inspiration writing this book.

To see those marvels on internet, you can go here: www.batini.com

You can also send comments, suggestions or info requests to: books@batini.com

Lucilio Batini

Index

Pink Floyd

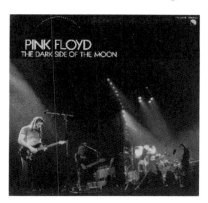

Vinyl LP

http://www.batini.com/pinkfloydjapanlp/

Stock

Stock Red

Sample

OP-8229 The Piper at the Gates of Dawn **1st Press 1967**

Obi ¥2200

Stock ¥2000   Stock Red   Stock ¥2200

OP-80281 The Piper at the Gates of Dawn **2ⁿᵈ / 3ʳᵈ Press 1970**

Was pressed in 2 different moments, in 1970 with ¥2000 and in 1974 with ¥2200 price,
difference on obi and back cover (price) and on labels (* or **)

Stock   Sample

EMS-80317 The Piper at the Gates of Dawn **4th Press 1974**

Stock   Sample

EMS-50104 The Piper at the Gates of Dawn **5th Press 1983**

Stock

Stock Red

Sample Red

OP-8743 A Saucerful of Secrets **1st Press 1968**

Obi ¥2200

Stock ¥2000   Stock Red   Stock ¥2200

OP-80282 A Saucerful of Secrets **2nd / 3rd Press 1970**

Was pressed in 2 different moments, in 1970 with ¥2000 and in 1974 with ¥2200 price,
difference on obi and back cover (price) and on labels (* or **)

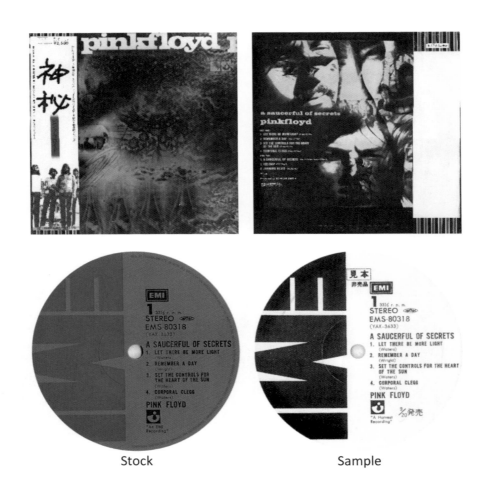

Stock   Sample

EMS-80318 A Saucerful of Secrets **4th Press 1974**

Stock   Stock Red   Sample Red

OP-8843 Soundtrack from The Film More **1st Press 1969**

Obi ¥2200

Stock ¥2000   Stock Red   Stock ¥2200

Sample Red

OP-80165 Soundtrack from The Film More **2nd / 3rd Press 1970**

Was pressed in 2 different moments, in 1970 with ¥2000 and in 1974 with ¥2200 price,
difference on obi and back cover (price) and on labels (* or **)

Stock   Sample

EMS-80319 Soundtrack from The Film More **4th Press 1974**

Obi ¥4400

Stock ¥4000

Sample Red

Stock ¥4400

Advance

OP-8912.3 Ummagumma 1st / 2nd Press 1970

Was pressed in 2 different moments, in 1970 with ¥4000 and in 1974 with ¥4400 price,
difference on obi and back cover (price) and on labels (* or **).
Advance press has only 1st record, Sample Red.

Stock   Sample

EMS-67043.44 Ummagumma **3rd Press 1974**

Stock   Sample

EMS-40070.71 Ummagumma **4th Press 1978**

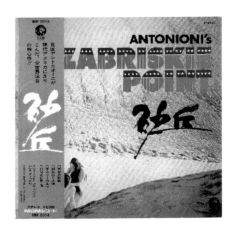  

Obi ¥2300

Stock

Sample

MM 2014 Zabriskie Point **1st / 2nd Press 1970**

Was pressed in 2 different moments, in 1970 with ¥2000 and in 1977 with ¥2300 price, difference on obi and back cover.

Stock   Sample

MMF 1012 Zabriskie Point **2nd Press 1977**

Obi ¥2200

Stock ¥2000

Stock Red

Stock ¥2200

Test Pressing

Sample Red

OP-80102 Atom Heart Mother **1ˢᵗ / 2ⁿᵈ Press 1970**

Was pressed in 2 different moments, in 1970 with ¥2000 and in 1974 with ¥2200 price,
difference on obi and back cover (price) and on labels (* or **)

Stock   Sample

EOZ-80008 Atom Heart Mother **Quadrophonic Press 1974**

Obi ¥2348

Stock   Sample

EMS-80320 Atom Heart Mother **3rd Press 1974**

Was also pressed later with ¥2348 price on obi due to changes in taxes rules.

Japan Sticker

MFSL 1-202 Atom Heart Mother **Original Master Recording 1994**

Obi ¥2200

Stock ¥2000   Stock Red   Stock ¥2200

Sample

OP-80261 Relics 1st / 2nd Press 1971

Was pressed in 2 different moments, in 1971 with ¥2000 and in 1974 with ¥2200 price,
difference on obi and back cover (price) and on labels (* or **)

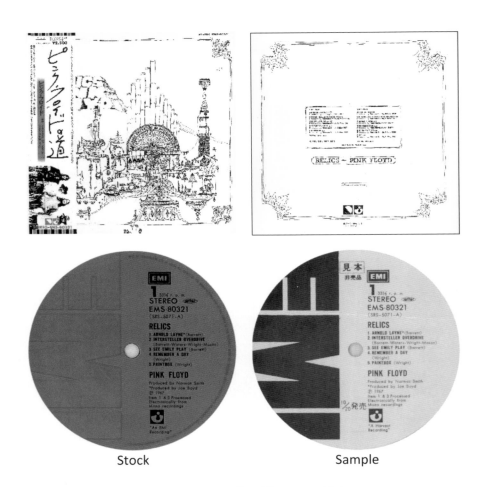

Stock   Sample

EMS-80321 Relics **3rd Press 1974**

PRP32 Promotional Copy **Promo 1972**

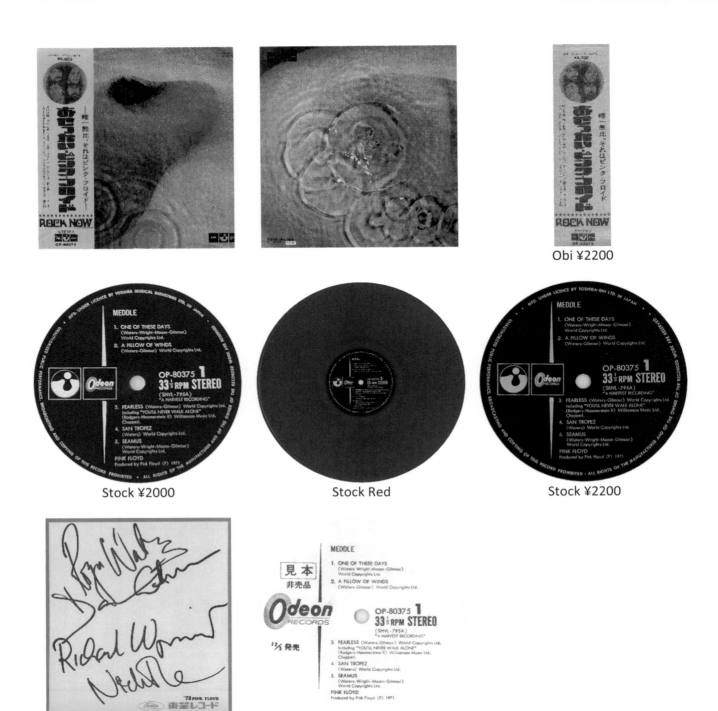

Obi ¥2200

Stock ¥2000

Stock Red

Stock ¥2200

Promo Sheeet

Sample

OP-80375 Meddle 1ˢᵗ / 2ⁿᵈ Press 1971

Was pressed in 2 different moments, in 1971 with ¥2000 and in 1974 with ¥2200 price,
difference on obi and back cover (price) and on labels (* or **)

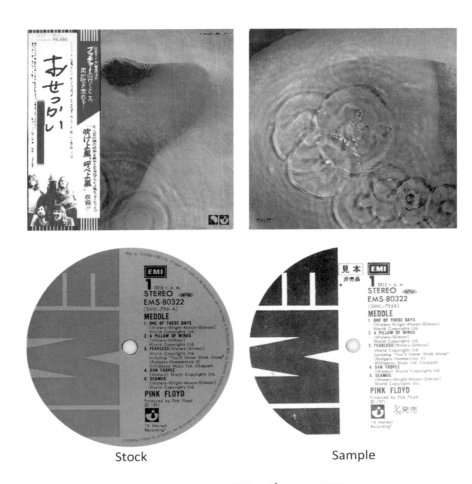

Stock   Sample

EMS-80322 Meddle **3rd Press 1974**

Obi ¥2200

Stock ¥2000   Sample   Stock ¥2200

EOP-80575 Obscured by Clouds **1st / 2nd Press 1972**

Was pressed in 2 different moments, in 1972 with ¥2000 and in 1974 with ¥2200 price,
difference on obi and back cover (price) and on labels (* or **)

Stock   Sample

EMS-80323 Obscured by Clouds **3**rd **Press 1974**

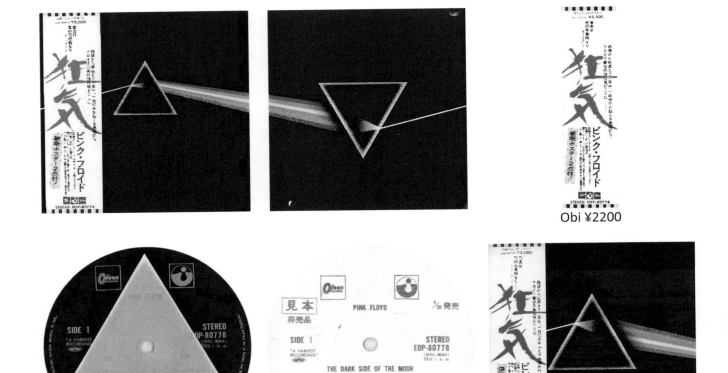

Obi ¥2200

Stock   Sample   Sample

EOP-80778 The Dark Side of the Moon **1ˢᵗ / 2ⁿᵈ Press 1973**

Was pressed in 2 different moments, in 1973 with ¥2000 and in 1974 with ¥2200 price on obi.
Early press (Sample) has the cover printed upside down.

Stock   Sample

EMZ-82005 The Dark Side of the Moon **Quadrophonic 1974**

Stock   Sample

EMLF-97002 The Dark Side of the Moon Pro Use Series 1978

 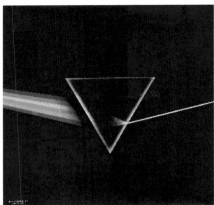 

Obi ¥2348

Stock   Sample

EMS-80324 The Dark Side of the Moon **3rd Press 1974**

Was also pressed later with ¥2348 price on obi due to changes in taxes rules.

Stock   Test Pressing

HW5149 The Dark Side of the Moon **Club Edition 1978**

Stock   Sample

EOP-93129B A nice Pair 1st Press 1974

Stock   Sample

EMS-40068.69 A nice Pair 2nd Press 1978

Stock   Sample

SOPO-100 Wish You Were Here **1ˢᵗ Press 1975**

25AP 1258 Wish You Were Here **2ⁿᵈ Press 1978**

25AP 1258 Wish You Were Here **3ʳᵈ Press 1978 Clear Plastic Wrap**

Stock	Sample	Test Pressing

30AP 1875 Wish You Were Here **Master Sound 1980**

Obi ¥2348

Stock

Sample

Test Pressing

Test Pressing

25AP 340 Animals 1977

Was also pressed later with ¥2348 price on obi due to changes in taxes rules.

Shop Sticker

Stock

Sample

Test Pressing

40AP 1750.1 The Wall 1979

XDAP 7 The Wall DJ Copy **Promo 1979**

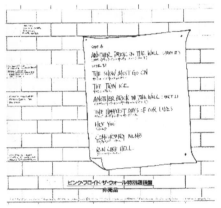

XDAP 93012 The Wall in Store **Promo 1979**

Stock   Sample

25AP 2260 A Collection of Great Dance Songs **1981**

Stock   Sample

30AP 2265 A Collection of Great Dance Songs **Master Sound 1981**

Stock   Sample

EMS-81600 Works 1983

Stock   Sample

25AP 2410 The Final Cut **1983**

Stock   Sample

30AP 2534 The Final Cut **1983**

Promo Booklet

Stock   Sample

28AP 3405 A Momentary Lapse of Reason **1987**

Pink Floyd

Vinyl LP Remastered

http://www.batini.com/pinkfloydjapanlp/

SIJP 11 The Piper at the Gates of Dawn **Remastered 2016**

SIJP 12 A Saucerful of Secrets **Remastered 2016**

SIJP 13 Soundtrack from The Film More **Remastered 2016**

SIJP 14.5 Ummagumma Remastered 2016

SIJP 16 Atom Heart Mother Remastered 2016

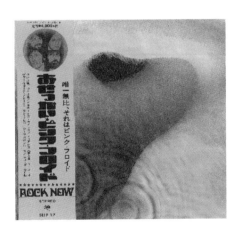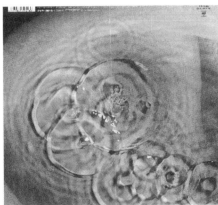

SIJP 17 Meddle Remastered 2016

SIJP 18 Obscured by Clouds **Remastered 2016**

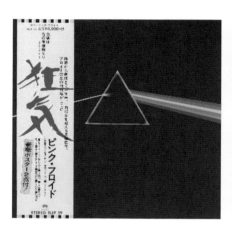

SIJP 19 The Dark Side of the Moon **Remstered 2016**

SIJP 20 Wish You Were Here **Remastered 2016**

SIJP 21 Animals **Remastered 2016**

SIJP 22.3 The Wall **Remastered 2016**

SIJP 24 The Final Cut **Remastered 2016**

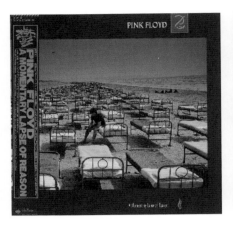

SIJP 25 A Momentary Lapse of Reason **Remastered 2016**

SIJP 111.2 A Momentary Lapse of Reason **Remastered 2021**

SIJP 26.7 The Division Bell **Remastered 2016**

Solos

Vinyl LP

http://www.batini.com/pinkfloydjapanlp/

Obi ¥2200

Stock ¥2000   Sample Red   Stock ¥2200

OP-8927 Syd Barrett, The Madcap Laughs **1ˢᵗ / 2ⁿᵈ Press 1970**

Was pressed in 2 different moments, in 1970 with ¥2000 and in 1974 with ¥2200 price, difference on obi and back cover (price) and on labels (* or **).

Stock   Sample

EMS-80636 Syd Barrett, The Madcap Laughs **3rd Press 1976**

It exists with 2 different color writing on ear, white and red.

EMS-50127 Syd Barrett, The Madcap Laughs **4th Press 1980**

Obi ¥2200

Stock ¥2000

Stock Red

Stock ¥2200

Sample Red

OP-80173 Syd Barrett, Barrett **1st / 2nd Press 1970**

Was pressed in 2 different moments, in 1970 with ¥2000 and in 1974 with ¥2200 price, difference on obi and back cover (price) and on labels (* or **).

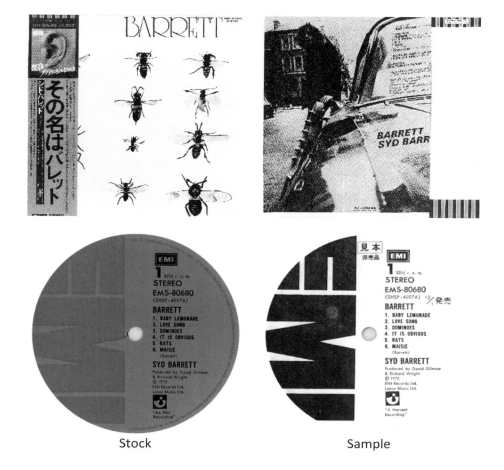

Stock   Sample

EMS-80680 Syd Barrett, Barrett **3rd Press 1976**

It exists with 2 different color writing on ear, white and red.

EMS-50128 Syd Barrett, Barrett **4th Press 1980**

Stock   Sample

EMS-67014.15 Syd Barrett, Syd Barrett **1975**

Stock   Sample

25AP 1077 David Gilmour, David Gilmour **1978**

Stock   Sample

28AP 2826 David Gilmour, About Face **1984**

Stock   Sample

25AP 2047 Nick Mason's Fictitious Sports **1981**

Stock   Sample

28AP 3075 Nick Mason / Rick Fenn, Profiles **1985**

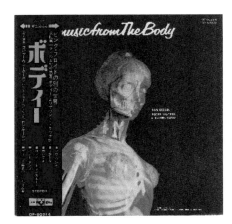
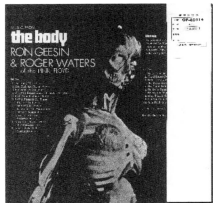

Obi ¥2200

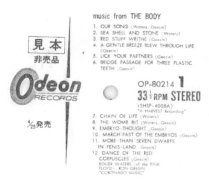

Stock ¥2000   Sampler   Stock ¥2200

OP-80214 Roger Waters / Ron Geesin, Music from The Body **1st / 2nd Press 1970**

Was pressed in 2 different moments, in 1970 with ¥2000 and in 1974 with ¥2200 price, difference on obi and back cover (price) and on labels (* or **).

Stock   Sample

EMS-80637 Roger Waters / Ron Geesin, Music from The Body **3rd Press 1976**

It exists with 2 different color writing on ear, white and red.

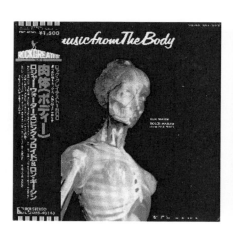

EMS-40143 Roger Waters / Ron Geesin, Music from The Body **4th Press 1980**

Stock   Sample

28AP 2875 Roger Waters, The Pros and Cons of Hitch-Hiking **1984**

Stock   Sample

30AP 2877 Roger Waters, The Pros and Cons of Hitch-Hiking **Master Sound 1984**

Stock   Sample

28VB-1139 OST, When the Wind Blows **1986**

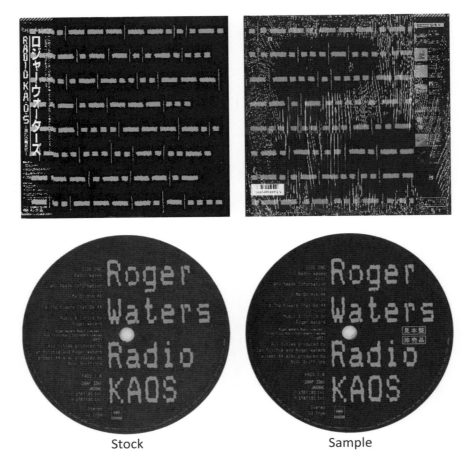

Stock   Sample

28AP 3361 Roger Waters, Radio Kaos **1987**

SIJP 70.1 Is this the Life we Really Want **2019**

Stock   Sample

25AP 1141 Richard Wright, Wet Dream **1978**

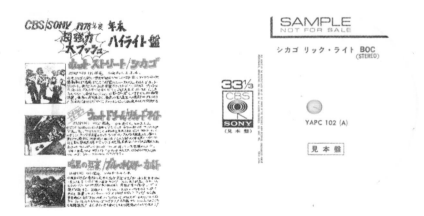

YAPC 102 Richard Wright / Chicago / Blue Oyster Cult, CBS / Sony **Promo 1978**

Various Artists

Vinyl LP

Stock   Sample Red   Test Pressing

OP-8798 Heavy 1968
(A2: Let There Be More Light / B2: Set The Controls for the Heart of the Sun)

JA101 Power Hits **1973**
(B10: Julia Dream)

JA101.202 Superstars of the 70s **1973**
(B10: Julia Dream)

MIS 1017 The Soundtrack Special 7 **1976**
(B4: Heart Beat, Pig Meat)

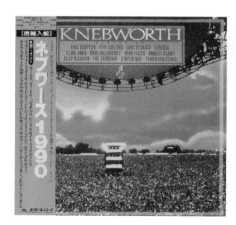

UK   NL

POJP 9001.2 Knebworth **1990**
UK / NL print with Japan Obi
(D4: Comfortably Numb / D5: Run Like Hell)

Various Artists

Vinyl LP Promo

http://www.batini.com/pinkfloydjapanlpvarious/

 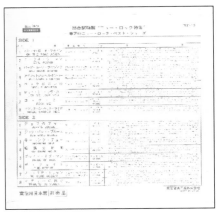 

PRP-13 Rock Generation **1968**

(B2: Jug Band Blues)

PRP-21 Popular Music Hilight **1970**

(B5: Set the Controls for the Heart of the Sun)

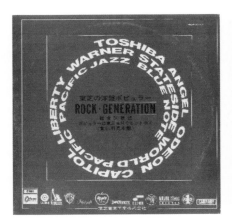  

PRP-22.3 Rock Generation **1970**

(A6: Careful with That Axe, Eugene)

PRP-27.28 Rock Now **1970**
(A2: Summer 68)

PRP-30.31 Rock Now **1970**
(D5: Summer 68)

PRP-34.35 Rock Now / Modern Soul **1970**
(A4: Julia Dream)

 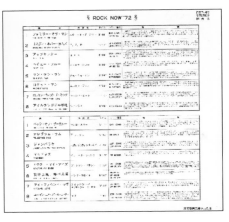 

PRP-43 Rock Now 72 **1972**

(B6: One of These Days)

 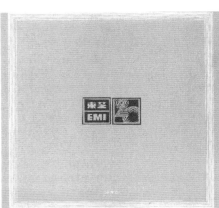 

TO-20-1.2 20th Anniversary Toshiba-EMI **1972**

(C8: One of These Days)

YALC 51 Powerful Highlight Disc **1975**
(A10: Have a Cigar)

YAPC 77 Popular Best 101 volume 1 **1975**
(A23: Have a Cigar, truncated)

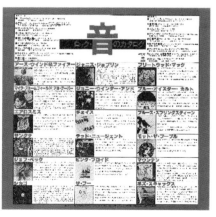

YAPC 105 Rock Best 100 **1976**
(B2: Have a Cigar)

XAAP 90009 All American Top 100 vol 21 **1980**
(A2: Another Brick in the Wall part 2)

XAAP 90010 All American Top 100 vol 22 **1980**
(A1: Another Brick in the Wall part 2)

XAAP 90011 All American Top 100 vol 23 **1980**
(A1: Another Brick in the Wall part 2)

XAAP 90012 All American Top 100 vol 24 **1980**
(A1: Another Brick in the Wall part 2)

XAAP 90013 All American Top 100 vol 25 **1980**
(A3: Another Brick in the Wall part 2)

XAAP 90019 All American Top 100 Extra **1980**
(A1: Another Brick in the Wall part 2)

XAAP 90020 All American Top 100 vol 32 **1981**
(B3: Another Brick in the Wall part 2)

XDAP 93009 Warmer Sound Special **1980**
(B3: Another Brick in the Wall part 2)

XDAP 93014 Super 5 **1980**
(A6: Another Brick in the Wall part 2)

XAAS 90002 CBS Sony Hilights **1980**
(B2: Another Brick in the Wall part 2)

XAAS 90006 CBS Sony Hilights **1980**
(B6: Comfortably Numb)

XAAP 90061 Summer Campaign 83 **1983**
(B3: Not Now John)

XDAP 93175 American Hit Tunes 16 **1987**
(A4: Learning to Fly)

XDAP 93106 Wall American Top 100 vol 61 **1984**
(B5: David Gilmour, Blue Light)

XAAP 90078 Big Hit on CBS Sony **1985**
(B5: Nick Mason, Lie for a Lie)

XDAP 93169 American Hit tunes vol 14 **1987**
(B3: Roger Waters, Radio Waves)

XDAP 93173 American Hit tunes vol 15 **1987**
(B6: Roger Waters, Radio Waves)

Pink Floyd

Vinyl LP Bootleg

http://www.batini.com/pinkfloydjapanlpother/

Posters

KP339-344 Live "Tokyo Triple" **1973**
(Osaka, Japan, 09/08/1971)

TPL3003 Live "Peace" **1975**
(Hakone, Japan, 06/08/1971)

1. careful with that axe, eugene
   cymbaline
2. embryo
   set the controls for the heart
   of the sun
3. saucerful of secret
4. atom heart mother

Pink Floyd

OG 719.720 Live "Spread Legs" **1974**
(Hamburg, Germany, 25/02/1971)

OG 745.746 Best of Tour 72-73 **1974**
(London, United Kingdom, 20/02/1972)

JL-511 Europe 74 1976
(London, United Kingdom, 17/11/1974)

JL-518 California Jammin 1976
(Fillmore West, USA, 29/04/1970)

PF-3077 AB Giant Barn Dance **1977**
(Wembley, United Kingdom, 15/03/1977)

PF-3077 CD 30KW P.A. **1977**
(Wembley, United Kingdom, 15/03/1977)

427-V The Wall Show in New York 80 **1981**
(New York, USA, 26/02/1980))

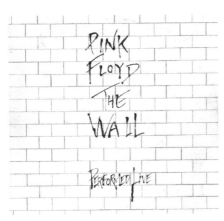 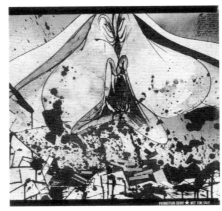

427-V The Wall Performed Live **1982**
(New York, USA, 26/02/1980)

PF71131.2 Delusions of Maturity **1988**
(Atlanta, USA, 03/11/1987)

White Cover

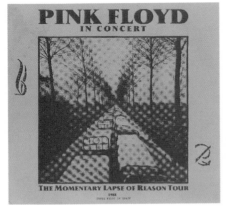

Brown Cover

PF-8321.3 Still First in Space 1990
(Tokyo, Japan, 02/03/1988)

N852 David Gilmour, About Face Live **1986**
(Quebec, Canada, 09/05/1984)

This Side

Stereo
33⅓ r.p.m.
Not For Sale

Welcome To The Machine
Have A Cigar
Wish You Were Here
Pigs On The Wing
In The Flesh ?

Other Side

XL1589
XL1589B

Set The Controls
For The Heart Of The Sun
Money
If

XL1589.90 Roger Waters / David Gilmour, Money **1985**
(RW: London, United Kingdom, 21/06/1984)
(DG: Los Angeles, USA, 22/06/1984)

MS-3002 Roger Waters, Earls Court **1984**
(London, United Kingdom, 21/06/1984)

Pink Floyd

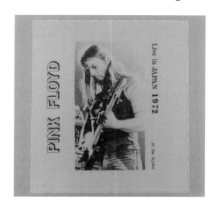

Acetate LP Bootleg

MM-112.3 Live In Santa Monica 1970 **1981**
(Los Angeles, USA, 23/10/1970)

Double LP pressed in 2 single discs, numbered on cover

Red

PC-012.3 Live In Italy At Palasport 1971 **1982**
(Brescia, Italy, 19/06/1971)

Double LP pressed in 2 single discs, numbered on cover

Stock

Stock Red

Sample Red

OR-2387 Let There be More Light / Remember a Day **1968**

2nd Cover

Stock

Sample

Test Pressing

OR-2715 The Nile Song / Main Theme **1969**

Stock

Stock Red

Sample

Yuusen Cable Radio Acetate

OR-2840 Julia Dream / Summer 68 **1971**

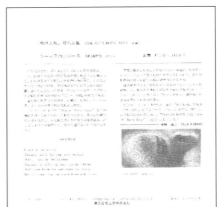

Stock

Stock Red

Sample Red

Stock 2ⁿᵈ

吹けよ風、呼べよ嵐

ピンク・フロイド

Yuusen Cable Radio Acetate

OR-2935 One of These Days / Seamus **1971**

Was repressed later with ** on label.

TV Advertising

Stock

Stock

EMR-20388 One of These Days / Seamus **1977**

Repressed later with TV advertising on cover.

Stock

Sample

Stock 2nd

OR-2935 "Big Four": One Of These Days / Julia Dream / Point Me To The Sky / See Emily Play **1971**

Repressed later with ** on label.

Stock   Sample

OR-2979 Point me at the Sky / Arnold Layne 1972

Stock   Stock Red   Sample

EOR-10149 Free Four / Absolutely Curtains **1972**

4RS-322 Free Four / Absolutely Curtains **1972 Promo**

Stock   Sample

SOPB 347 Have a Cigar / Welcome to the Machine **1975**

Stock

Sample

Yuusen Cable Radio Acetate

06SP 453 Another Brick in the Wall part 2 / One of my Turns 1979

Stock   Sample

07SP 491 Comfortably Numb / Hey You **1980**

Stock   Sample

07SP 647 Not Now John / The Hero's Return **1983**

XDSP 93036 Not Now John / Your Possible Pasts **1983 Promo**

Stock

Sample

07SP 1060 Learning to Fly / Terminal Frost **1987**

XDSP 93094 Learning to Fly / Terminal Frost **1987 Promo**

HIT-1467 Michel Magne: Le Jeu de l Amour / Do You Want Marry Me **1967**

Note: David Gilmour Vocal on B Side.

Pink Floyd

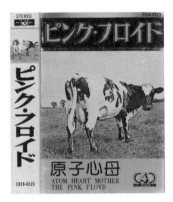

Audio Tape

ZR23-463 A Saucerful of Secrets **Reprint**

ZR23-464 More Reprint

EOZT-3060 Ummagumma **1969**

ZR36-467 Ummagumma **Reprint**

OZA-3155 Atom Heart Mother **1970**

EOZA-3523 Atom Heart Mother **Quadrophonic**

ZR25-184 Atom Heart Mother **Reprint**

OYA-7286 Atom Heart Mother **8 Track**

OXA-5067 Atom Heart Mother **Reel**

ZR23-465 Relics Reprint

OZA-3210 Meddle **1971**

ZR25-185 Meddle **Reprint**

OZA-3210 Meddle **Reel**

ZR23-466 Obscured by Clouds **Reprint**

OZA-3210 Meddle **Reel**

EMZA-3534 The Dark Side of the Moon **Quadrophonic**

ZR28-365 The Dark Side of the Moon **Dynasound**

Type 1

Type 2

ZR25-186 The Dark Side of the Moon **Reprint**

EOYA-7440 The Dark Side of the Moon **8 Track**

EMYA-7534 The Dark Side of the Moon **8 Track Quadrophonic**

EOYT-7083 A Nice Pair **8 Track**

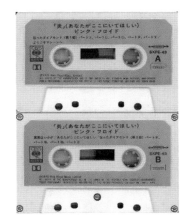

SKPE-43 Wish You Were Here **1975**

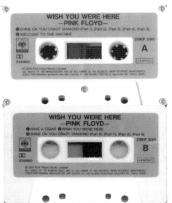

25KP 530 Wish You Were Here **Reprint**

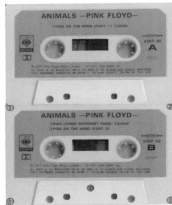

25KP 90 Animals 1977

40KP 531 The Wall **1979**

XDKP 93003 The Wall in Store **1979 Promo**

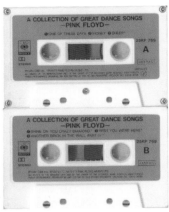

25KP 769 A Collection of Great Dance Songs **1981**

ZR25-900 Works 1981

25KP 845 The Final Cut **1983**

28KP 1535 A Momentary Lapse of Reason **1987**

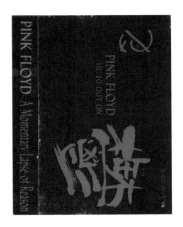

A Momentary Lapse of Reason **1987 Promo**

42KP 5294.5 A Momentary Lapse of Reason **1988**

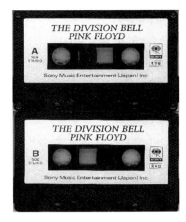

SRCS 7324 The Division Bell **1994 Promo**

PINK FLOYD
"p・u・l・s・e"

SRCS 7651

1995.6.6 ON SALE   2枚組 ¥4,200(Tax Incl.)

PINK FLOYD / p・u・l・s・e

SRCS 7651

Sony Records
Sony Music Entertainment (Japan) Inc.

NOT FOR SALE

SIDE B
7. HEY YOU
8. A GREAT DAY FOR FREEDOM
9. SORROW
10. HIGH HOPES
11. ANOTHER BRICK IN THE WALL (PART TWO)
12. ONE OF THESE DAYS

SIDE A
1. SHINE ON YOU CRAZY DIAMOND
2. ASTRONOMY DOMINE
3. WHAT DO YOU WANT FROM ME
4. LEARNING TO FLY
5. KEEP TALKING
6. COMING BACK TO LIFE

PINK FLOYD
"p・u・l・s・e"

SRCS 7652

1995.6.6 ON SALE   2枚組 ¥4,200(Tax Incl.)

PINK FLOYD / p・u・l・s・e

SRCS 7652

Sony Records
Sony Music Entertainment (Japan) Inc.

NOT FOR SALE

SIDE A
1. SPEAK TO ME
2. BREATHE
3. ON THE RUN
4. TIME
5. THE GREAT GIG IN THE SKY
6. MONEY
7. US AND THEM
8. ANY COLOUR YOU LIKE
9. BRAIN DAMAGE
10. ECLIPSE

SIDE B
11. WISH YOU WERE HERE
12. COMFORTABLY NUMB
13. RUN LIKE HELL

SRCS 7651.2 Pulse 1995 Promo

TOCP-65356.57 Is there anybody out there? **2000 Promo**

TOCP-65910.11 Echoes 2001 Promo

Solos

Audio Tape

25KP 318 David Gilmour **1978**

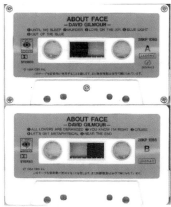

28KP 1085 David Gilmour, About Face **1984**

28KP 1125 Roger Waters, The Pros and Cons of Hitch Hiking **1984**

28KP 1526 Roger Waters, Radio Kaos **1987**

SRCS 5913 Roger Waters, Amused to Death **1992 Promo**

ロジャー・ウォーターズ / イン・ザ・フレッシュ

Roger Waters / In The Flesh

PINKの全盛期から遂に解放された、ROGER WATERSへ遊説!!
8年ぶりとなるアルバムは、2000年のツアーを内容初ライブアルバム。
ピンク・フロイドに永遠のマスター・ピースの数々から多数曲「Each Small Candle」まで全24曲収録1!

DISC-1

Side-A

1. "In The Flesh" イン・ザ・フレッシュ (from ザ・ウォール)
2. "The Happiest Days Of Our Lives"
   ザ・ハピエスト・デイズ・オブ・アワ・ライヴス (from ザ・ウォール)
3. "Another Brick In The Wall, Part2"
   アナザー・ブリック・イン・ザ・ウォール(パート2)(from ザ・ウォール)
4. "Mother" マザー (from ザ・ウォール)
5. "Get Your Filthy Hands Off My Desert"
   ゲット・ユア・フィルシィ・ハンズ・オフ・マイ・デザート (from ファイナル・カット)
6. "Southampton Dock"
   サウザンプトン・ドック (from ファイナル・カット)
7. "Pigs On The Wing, Part 1"
   翼持つ豚 パート1 (from アニマルズ)
8. "Does" ドゥ (from アニマルズ)

Side-B

9. "Welcome To The Machine" ようこそマシーンへ (from 炎)
10. "Wish You Were Here" あなたがここにいてほしい (from 炎)
11. "Shine On You Crazy Diamond (Parts 1-8)"
    クレイジー・ダイアモンド(パート1-8)(from 炎)
12. "Set The Controls For The Heart Of The Sun"
    太陽賛歌 (from 神秘)

SRCS-2393~2394 / 2000.12.27(予定) 2枚組 / ¥3,780(Tax In)

Sony Music Entertainment(Japan)Inc. **SMe** RECORDS.
<お問い合わせ> SMEインターナショナル ☎ 03-5792-7562

DISC-2

Side-A

1. "Breath (In The Air)" 生命の息吹き (from 狂気)
2. "Time" タイム (from 狂気)
3. "Money" マネー (from 狂気)
4. "Pros and Cons of Hitch Hiking Part 11
   (aka 5:06 a.m. – Every Stranger's Eyes)"
   完全なる 5:06 a.m. ストレンジャー・5時 (mumb)ヒッチハイクの賛否両論)
5. "Perfect Sense (Parts I and II)"
   完全意思 パート I & II (from 死滅遊戯)
6. "The Bravery Of Being Out Of Range"
   勇気なき報道 (from 死滅遊戯)
7. "It's A Miracle" 奇跡 (from 死滅遊戯)

Side-B

8. "Amused To Death" 死滅遊戯 (from 死滅遊戯)
9. "Brain Damage" 狂人は心に (from 狂気)
10. "Eclipse" 狂気日食 (from 狂気)
11. "Comfortably Numb" コンフォタブリー・ナム (from ザ・ウォール)
12. "Each Small Candle" イーチ・スモール・キャンドル (new song)

SRCS 2393.4 Roger Waters, In the Flesh **2000 Promo**

SICP 122 Roger Waters, Flickering Flame **2002 Promo**

SICP 695 Roger Waters, To Kill the Child **2004**

Various Artists

Audio Tape

http://www.batini.com/pinkfloydjapantape/

8 Track

Cassette

OYP-1097 Various Artists, Heavy **1968**
(S1/2: Let There Be More Light)
(S2/2: Set the Control for the Heart of the Sun)

8 Track

8 Track

Cassette

Various Artists, Tape 8-6
1973 Promo
(P3/4: Speak To Me)
(P3/5: Breathe)

PYA-879
Various Artists
Rock Now 74
1974 Promo
(P3/2: Money)

XAKP 90037
Various Artists
Big Hit on CBS
Sony 1985-10
1985 Promo
(S2/5: NM: Lie for a Lie)

Semi Official

Audio Tape

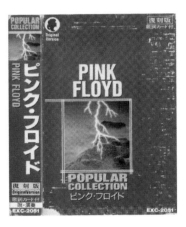

EXC-2051 Popular Collection **1988**

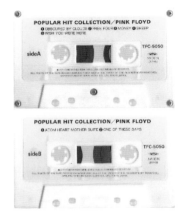

TFC-5050 Popular Hit Collection

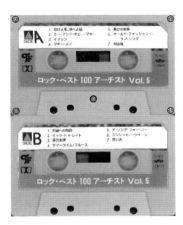

TC-1053 Various Artists, Rock Best 100 Artists 5
(S1/1: One of These Days)

TFC-7009 Various Artists Progressive Rock
(S1/2: Money)

GOGO-2 Various Artists, Go Go Festival 2
(S1/2: Money)

CS-015 Various Artists, Rock Best Omnibus 15 **1989**
(S2/1: Money)

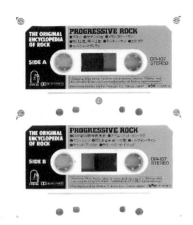

DR-107 Various Artists, The Encyclopedia of Rock
(S1/1: Money)

Pink Floyd

Video Tape

http://www.batini.com/pinkfloydjapanvhs/

Type 1 & 2

TE-M507 Pompei **VHS**

TE-M507 Pompei **Betamax**

104 Pompei **VHS Promo**

104 Pompei **Betamax Promo**

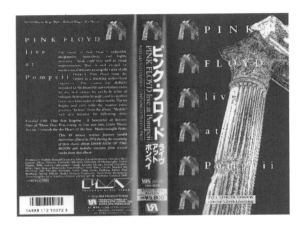

VAH-0072 Pompei **VHS Reprint 1ˢᵗ**

POVP-1503 Pompei **VHS Reprint 2ⁿᵈ**

VAVZ-2046 Live at Pompei **VHS Reprint 3ʳᵈ**

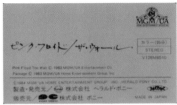

V128-M8510 The Wall **VHS 1984**

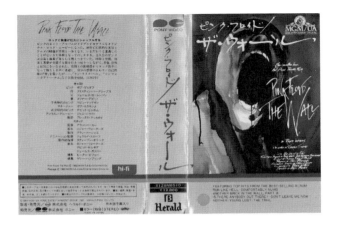

X128-M8510 The Wall **Betamax 1984**

V128F8709 The Wall **VHS 1987**

PCVM 10020 The Wall VHS 1989

WV-50268 The Wall VHS 1994

Stock & Promo

SRVM 1547 The Wall VHS 1999

42ZP 136 In Concert **VHS**

CSWM 6757 In Concert **Hi8**

Stock & Promo

SRVM 1505 Pulse VHS

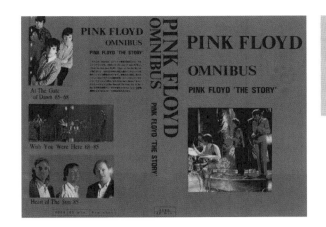

4066 Omnibus VHS Bootleg

Solos

Video Tape

http://www.batini.com/pinkfloydjapanvhs

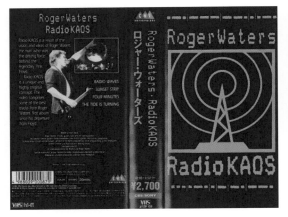

27ZP 132 Roger Waters, Radio Kaos **VHS**

27QP 132 Roger Waters, Radio Kaos **Betamax**

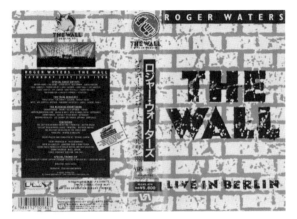

Stock & Promo

VAVP-180 Roger Waters, Live in Berlin **VHS 1st**

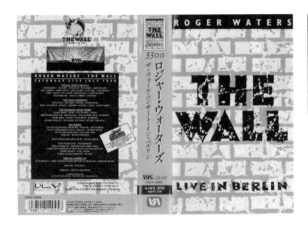

VAVZ-2045 Roger Waters, Live in Berlin **VHS 2nd**

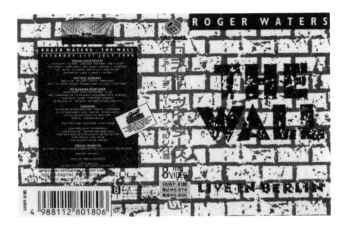

VAWP-8180 Roger Waters, Live in Berlin **Hi8**

 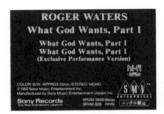

SRVM 828 Roger Waters, What God Wants 1 **VHS**

Promo Only

PINK FLOYD
" HIGH HOPES "

Sony Records
Sony Music Entertainment (Japan) Inc.

ROGER WATERS
An Interview about
"To Kill A Child" & "Leaving Beirut"

NOT FOR SALE

Video Tape

http://www.batini.com/pinkfloydjapanvhs

PINK FLOYD " HIGH HOPES "
Sony Records
Sony Music Entertainment (Japan) Inc.

PINK FLOYD
店頭演奏用ビデオ

ピンク・フロイド／ザ・ウォール
９４年３月１８日発売（サンプル）
ワーナー・ホーム・ビデオ

High Hopes / Instore Video **VHS Promo**

2003年９月10日発売
クラシック・アルバムズ：
VABG-1115¥4,700（税抜）
ピンク・フロイド／狂気
Color／16：9／Dolby Digital
VIDEOARTS MUSIC
Stereo／日本語字幕／約80分

VABG-1115 The Dark Side of the Moon Documentary **VHS Promo**

David Gilmour
「On An Island
(Special Edition)」
DVD

MHCP 1223 David Gilmour, On an Island **VHS Promo**

ROGER WATERS
An Interview about
"To Kill A Child" & "Leaving Beirut"

NOT FOR SALE

SICP 695 Roger Waters, To Kill the Child **VHS Promo**

Various Artists

Video Tape

http://www.batini.com/pinkfloydjapanvhs

TE-M525 Various Artists, Stamping Ground **VHS**
(Set the Controls for the Heart of the Sun)
(A Saucerful of Secrets)

V148-M2002 Superstars in Concert **VHS**
(18: Careful with That Axe, Eugene)

X148-M2002 Superstars in Concert **Betamax**
(18: Careful with That Axe, Eugene)

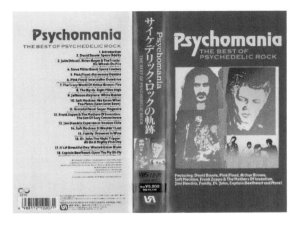

VAVJ-207 Various Artists, Psychomania **VHS 1ˢᵗ**
(5: Astronomy Domine)
(6: Interstellar Overdrive)

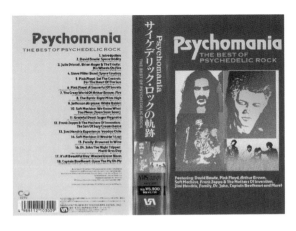

VAVJ-207 Various Artists, Psychomania **VHS 2ⁿᵈ**
(5: Set the Controls for the Heart of the Sun)
(6: A Saucerful of Secrets)

VAVZ-2086 Various Artists, Psychomania **VHS 3ʳᵈ**
(5: Set the Controls for the Heart of the Sun)
(6: A Saucerful of Secrets)

VAH-0111 Various Artists, Rock'n'roll 67 vol.1 **VHS**
(3: See Emily Play)

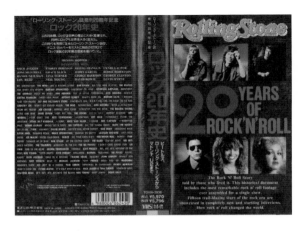

TOVW-3036 Various Artists, 20 Years of Rock'n'roll **VHS**
(Money)

VW-13857 Various Artists, The History of Rock'n'roll 70s vol.8 **VHS**

PCVE-10771 Various Artists, Eight Miles High **VHS**
(Arnold Layne, Astronomy Domine, Apples and Oranges)

NSW-2534A Various Artists, Eight Miles High **VHS**
(Arnold Layne, Astronomy Domine, Apples and Oranges)

TEVP-45027 Various Artists, Rock Aid Armenia **VHS**
(13: One Slip)

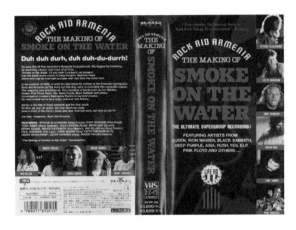

BVVP-26 Various Artists, The Making of Rock Aid Armenia **VHS**

APVG-4002 Various Artists, Knebworth vol.2 **VHS**
(16: Shine On You Crazy Diamond)
(17: Run Like Hell)

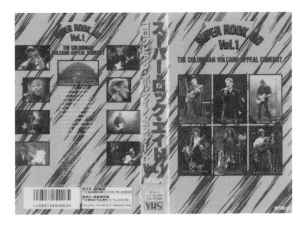

SFXV-12 Various Artists, Super Rock Aid vol.1 **VHS**
(5: DG: Run Like Hell)
(6: DG: Out of the Blue)
(7: DG: Comfortably Numb)

HM088-3156 Pete Townshend, Deep End **VHS**
(7: DG: Love on the Air)

VAVZ-2059 Various Artists, The Super Session IX **VHS**
(David Gilmour on Guitar)

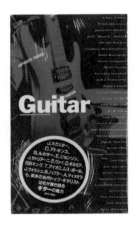  

V148-M2002 Superstars in Concert **VHS**
(David Gilmour on Guitar)

Movie

Video Tape

MVH-0045 More **VHS**

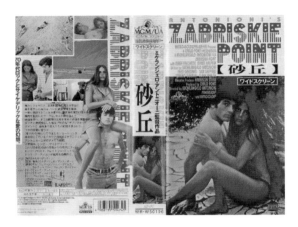

WR-W50196 Zabriskie Point **VHS**

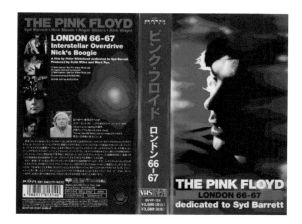

BVVP-124 London 66-67 **VHS**

TEVP-38043 Tonite, let's all make love in London **VHS 1st**

VPVU-67858 Tonite, let's all make love in London **VHS 2nd**

SRVM 822 La Carrera Panamericana **VHS**

PCVH-30084 Superstar, The Life and Times of Andy Warhol **VHS**

NJV-37208 White of the Eye **VHS**
(Nick Mason Soundtrack)

NAVA-10053 A Coeur Joie **VHS 1ˢᵗ**
(David Gilmour Vocal on a song of the OST)

VZ-1236 A Coeur Joie **VHS 2ⁿᵈ**
(David Gilmour Vocal on a song of the OST)

BES-1231 La Marge **VHS 1st**
(Wish You Were Here on the OST)

TH1892 La Marge **VHS 2nd**
(Wish You Were Here on the OST)

V128F8197 When the Wind Blows **VHS 1ˢᵗ**

PCVX-10114 When the Wind Blows **VHS 2ⁿᵈ**

JHF 0432 The Legend of 1900 **VHS**

JHF 0433 The Legend of 1900 **VHS**

Pink Floyd

Books

http://www.batini.com/pinkfloydjapanprogram/

Wish You Were Here

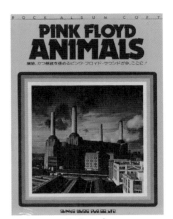

Animals

The Wall

Best Of

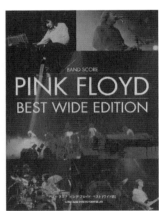

Best Wide

Pink Floyd Music Sheet

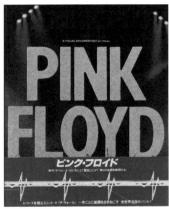

A Visual Documentary 1
By Miles

A Visual Documentary 2
By Miles

Story and Documentary

Biography

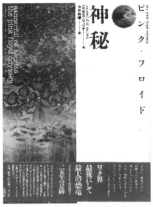

Odyssey

Lyrics

Live Tour In Japan

Pink Floyd Books

UK Progressive Rock '70
1

UK Progressive Rock '70
2

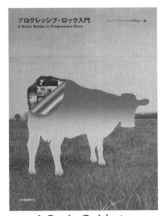

A Basic Guide to
Progressive Rock

Megalostage

Various Books

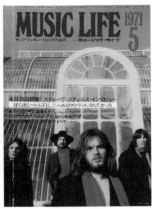

Music Life
1971.5

Zoo 3
1975.11

British Rock Magazine 7
2000.2

Discovery 2011

Magazines

Rockin Balls 6

Rockin Balls 8

Pink Fan 17

Fanzines

Pink Floyd

Paper

http://www.batini.com/pinkfloydjapanprogram/

Pompei 1972 Handbill

Tour **1972** Program

Program

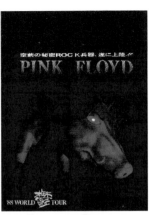

Program Promo

Book Promo

Tour **1988**

Sony Catalogue

Program

Handbill

Ticket

Hakone 1971

Program

Newsletter 71.12

Program

Best Seller 1973

Rock Now Promo 1971/1973

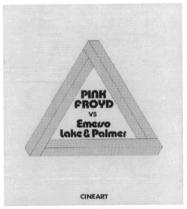

PF vs ELP Program

Perfect Bowl Handbill

Handbill

Handbill

Handbill

Pink Floyd

Promo Posters

http://www.batini.com/pinkfloydjapanprogram/

Odeon

Odeon

Odeon

Calendar Odeon 1974.01

Calendar Sony 1978.10

The Division Bell 1994

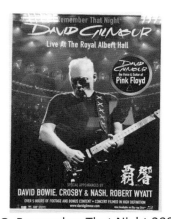

DG: Remember That Night 2007

DG: Rattle That Lock 2015

Promo Posters

Movie

Paper

Program

Handbill 1

Handbill 2

Poster 1

Poster 2

Postcards

More 1969

Program

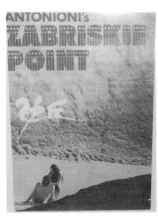

Poster

Book

Ticket

Zabriskie Point **1970**

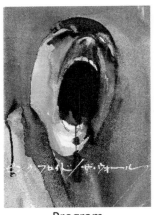

Program

Poster 1

Poster 2

Handbill

Tickets

The Wall Movie 1982

Program

Program

A Coeur Joie 1967

Program

Poster

La Marge 1975

Program

When The Wind Blows 1986

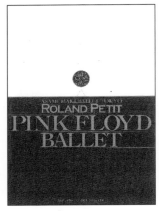

Program

Handbill

Roland Petit, Pink Floyd Ballet 2004

To be continued with Part 2: Digital…

Printed in Poland
by Amazon Fulfillment
Poland Sp. z o.o., Wrocław
14 August 2023